Esoterism and Symbol

Esoterism and Symbol

R.A. Schwaller de Lubicz

Translated
by
André and Goldian VandenBroeck

Inner Traditions International
One Park Street, Rochester, VT 05767

Inner Traditions International
One Park Street
Rochester, Vermont 05767
www.InnerTraditions.com

First U.S. Edition 1985

Esoterism and Symbol was first published in French under the title *Propos sur
Esotérisme et Symbole* by La Colombe, Editions du Vieux Colombier, Paris
1960.

© 1977 by Dervy-Livre

First English translation copyright © 1985
by Inner Traditions International Ltd.

20 19 18 17

LIBRARY OF CONGRESS CATALOGING IN PUBLICATION DATA
Schwaller de Lubicz, R. A.
    Esoterism and symbol.

    Translation of: Propos sur ésotérisme et symbole.
    1. Occult sciences.   2. Symbolism.   I. Title.
BF1439.S3813   1985   135.4   84-15771
ISBN 978-089281014-7

Printed and bound in the United States

CONTENTS

Esoterism has no common measure with deliberate concealment of the truth, that is, with secrecy in the conventional sense of the term.

If it were otherwise, writings such as the Egyptian Pyramid Texts, the Vedas and Upanishads of India, China's *Tao Te Ching*, the Genesis of Moses, the Gospels, the Revelations, and others, would have to be thought of as colossal mystifications.

It is inconceivable that scholars, philologists, theologians, and, in general, all those interested in the history of this world, should not as yet have understood the importance of the Pyramid Texts. No other scriptural texts, preserved and transmitted across the millennia because of their sacred nature, have reached us intact in form. Various transcriptions, translations, and commentaries, if they have not altered the fundamental meaning, at best leave room for doubt as to the original form, which is precisely the vehicle for esoterism.

Carved into stone, the writings in the chambers of the Fifth Dynasty pyramids have been preserved, unaltered, for four thousand years. The Samaritans treasure as a sacred relic a Bible they claim as "authentic," while here at the holy places of Egypt, ignorant but curious tourists brush carelessly against these carved stones where every feature—each line, each arrangement of text, each color—has a particular significance, there being no doubt that every detail is intentional.

Although we may not yet know how to interpret these words, let us at least preserve them for those who will come after us. Was it not greatly to the credit of Bonaparte's mission that it scrupulously copied texts which, at the time, no one yet knew how to decipher?

If the intention of the Gospels, for example, were to give to mankind a moral code for ordinary life, and if the way toward the "Father" were explicable in simple terms, then why hinder us from reaching this aim by speaking in parables? Why should all these writings hide what can be openly said in order to help the unhappy masses of this world? Was it through a perverse need to create a mystery, an "opiate for the masses," as the materialists say? Was it because the world of those days was so uncultured in comparison with ours, which is so highly intelligent? Would it be because those prophets and God-inspired men did not better know how to express themselves?

We have enough evidence of the intelligence, wisdom, and unquestionably high degree of civilization reached in the past to warrant dismissing such assumptions.

On the other hand, no cryptograph or riddle remains undecipherable. It is therefore naive to believe that such texts as ancient Egypt has left us in great profusion would base an esoteric meaning on a mystification of this sort, were such esoterism expressible by writing. In the composition of sacred texts, the cryptograph and the riddle never have any purpose other than to awaken the reader's attention, to place an accent on one aspect of the text, in short, to guide him toward the esoteric sense of the writing. The same applies to a play on words or a parable.

Esoterism can be neither written nor spoken, and hence cannot be betrayed. One must be prepared *to grasp it*, *to see it*, *to hear it*. This preparation is not a *knowing* but a *being-able*, and can ultimately be acquired only through the effort of the individual himself, by a struggle against all obstacles, and a victory over the human-animal nature.

There is a sacred science, and for thousands of years countless inquisitive people have sought in vain to penetrate its "secrets." It is as if they attempted to dig a hole in the sea with an ax. The tool must be of the same nature as the objective to be worked upon. Spirit is found only with spirit, and esoterism is the spiritual aspect of the world, inaccessible to cerebral intelligence.

Those who profess to reveal the esoterism of such teachings are charlatans. They may try to explain the implication of a certain word or formula as with a conventional secret, but with regard to sacred science, they will never be able to do more than put one word in place of another, and at best this will be bad literature replacing a simple idea.

The true initiate can guide a gifted pupil and help him to travel more quickly along the path to consciousness, and the pupil, upon reaching stages of illumination by his own inner light, will read the esoterism of such teaching directly. No one can do it for him.

There is in man a cerebral intelligence and also an innate intelligence called intelligence-of-the-heart. The latter comes into being through a fusion of the cosmic Cause which is contained in its materialization with the same Cause which is in us. This is possible because the nature of both Causes is identical.

As long as we are placed in duality before Nature, we judge it objectively. "Original sin" is the separation— hence the opposition—of complementary aspects whose merging makes for Unity, just as the superimposed colors red and green result in the "colorless."

In this Unity, our cerebral intelligence can no longer discern anything, and so has no further role to play. It needs opposition in order to function: we and the object, man and woman, yes and no, night and day, light and shade. Thus is every living organism constituted; a ceaseless oscillation between birth and death, increase and decrease.

The red rods and cones in the retina of the eye intercept the color green, neutralize this color, and excite a complementary reaction of the optic nerve, which *sees* green as opposed to red.

Thus the cerebral function is entirely based on a principle of crossing, as, for example, the right side of the brain generally controls the left side of the body. Likewise, a concrete image, the vision of an object, evokes its qualification or qualitative description. This is accomplished by abstract elements which are themselves the result of comparisons.

Conversely, it is impossible for cerebral intelligence to conceive an abstraction without defining it by a concrete image. But here we must be aware of distinguishing moments of cerebral intelligence from moments of intelligence-of-the-heart. We will return to this later. The origin of the universe being one single and unique source of energy, there is, owing to this common paternity, a communion among all things in the world. There is a kinship between a certain mineral and a plant and an animal and a man: They are linked by being of the "same nature," because in the final analysis, there is only a simple series of basic characteristics whence, by combinations, innumerable possibilities emerge. These can, however, be classified in a few large families and their subgroups.

Despite the variety of the races of humanity, each consisting of a multitude of very diverse individuals, all men are organized in essentially the same way. What distinguishes one from another is his state of consciousness and hence his mental control, his particular psychic and sexual life, and consequently his affinities.

The variable moment, therefore, is of an abstract order, but can be perfectly well observed and analyzed in its effects.

On the other hand, the abstract cause in a *state of genesis* within the concrete—and apparently stable— scheme of man's organic constitution, is beyond rational analysis. A totality of purely bodily experiences evidently maintains this genesis, but individual and group heredity play a part as well. Here again, one can speak of physiological adaptations transmitted by heredity, but the impulse toward this genesis must nevertheless still be provided by an incomprehensible moment which, in sum, could be called *formless concentration* in the transmitting seed. Our common origin is by no means remote. It does not take us back into the primeval darkness: It is present and constant in that man feeds directly or indirectly on all the kingdoms, and thus enters into constant exchange with their particular natures and, finally, by way of the mineral origin, with the cosmic energy from which everything arises.

It is completely impossible for our minds to conceive something which is not a part of concrete Nature and which we have not experienced through our bodily becoming. The dog cannot understand man; it can be aware of him physically, insofar as he is physical, but it can no more understand him than the mollusk can understand the horse or the plant the mollusk. Is it because they lack the necessary cerebral organ? Most certainly. But what brings about this organ? Does the plant thrusting upward have the mentality to understand the sky? Yet it makes no mistake. There is an innate intelligence which is precisely the *characteristic nature of the entity*. And man possesses this innate nature himself in the mineral of his bones, in the vegetal matter of the tissues of his organs, in the animal coordination of his organs, which together make up his laboratory of assimilation and transformation as an independent being. We define this innate intelligence too glibly by the word "instinct." We would do well to examine what comprises it and whence it comes.

Cerebral intelligence depends upon the senses, the recording of observed facts, and the comparison of ideas.

No element of cerebral intelligence is abstract, and every qualitative or abstract idea results from the comparison of concrete elements.

The cerebral organ is formed by stages. For this, the organism must develop three faculties: that of the senses, that which records observations, and that which compares the recorded ideas, namely, memory. *Reason*, about which we shall speak later, is of a different order. For now, we are still speaking only of the human animal. The senses are the organs by which the "principial elements" are perceived. Touch, the tactile sense, is of the Earth, that is, of everything forming a material obstacle to the matter of the body. The body of the wind is Earth, as is the body of water, or stone. The senses are aware of an activity only by opposing it with a resistance of identical nature. Taste is related to Water, and nothing, be it a gas or a solid, can be tasted unless it be slightly dissolved. Thus there is a Water principle in everything. The sense of smell belongs to Air because nothing can be smelled unless it be volatile, or made so, as, for example, by heat. And so there is an Air principle in all things. Sight belongs to Fire: nothing can be seen without the radiance of Fire, just as a piece of iron, dark in the darkness, becomes dull red and then dazzling white if heated by an invisible energy.

The heat of ordinary fire belongs to touch and not to sight. Thus the Fire principle exists in all visible things.

Hearing belongs to the quint-element, the Word, which becomes perceptible physically and tangibly through sound. The first four senses pass through the brain; the fifth sense, hearing, passes through the "heart" without speaking directly to the brain. It is the spiritual sense, the door to intelligence-of-the-heart.

Each thing has its own sound.

All things communicate with one another through the principial elements. The spheres to which our human genesis has not yet attained escape us, as long as we cannot transform them and reduce them to the principial element of the spheres of our inborn intelligence. All scientific instrumentation is but a reduction of this kind. There are aspects of Fire, Air, Water, and Earth which we have not yet experienced in the realms preceding us. It is therefore perfectly reasonable to admit the possible existence of a world interpenetrating the aspect of things now perceptible to us, a world composed of exactly the same principial elements, just as there are light waves which our eyes cannot perceive (infrared and ultraviolet). This still only concerns the possible expansion of the sensitivity of our senses, but the existence of the hearing faculty also allows us to believe in the existence of a *principial* or *ideal* state corresponding, like the principial elements, to principial *forms*.

The fact that there is in man, once he has passed beyond the simple human-animal stage, the possibility of conceiving abstractions which the cerebral intelligence cannot understand as such, demonstrates the existence of a world parallel to ours in constitution but entirely different in aspect, extent, and genesis. This genesis would then be a genesis of return, just as, from the source to ourselves, there is a genesis of bodily becoming.

Cerebral intelligence, which we see developed in the higher animal aspect of man, is strictly limited by the boundaries imposed on the senses. Intelligence-of-the-heart, to the contrary, is independent of them, and belongs to the great complex called life.

The fundamental character of cerebral intelligence is that it is born of duality, the complementing which may also be called the *sexualization of the universe*. Quality is comprehensible only through this opposition of complementaries; moreover, the idea of quality exists in Nature only, that is, in the dualized universe.

Quality defines quantity, and, inversely, quantity compared with another quantity defines quality. Any so-called abstract idea exists only if we can limit it by a quantity. We can be satisfied with words and say, for example, "horizon," or "axis," and construct sentences with these words, but as soon as we try to analyze their meanings, we are bound to make them objective: otherwise, our cerebral ability comes to a halt. An abstraction must be made concrete or else it will be impossible for us to understand.

The word "axis" is a typical example, since this idea, which we qualify as imaginary, cannot be imagined, that is, made objective. Yet the axis (not to be confused with "axle") is a fundamental characteristic of every rotating body. This again confirms the probability of an intelligence different from that of our cerebral possibilities since our corporeal world shows us the indisputable existence of functions and even of forms which unquestionably exist, and yet always have been and will remain entirely beyond the grasp of this single cerebral instrument alone.

We have borrowed the term "intelligence-of-the-heart" from the ancient Egyptians in order to designate that other aspect of man which allows us to penetrate beyond our animal limits and which, in truth, makes for human man's characteristic progression toward divine Man: the awakening of this original principle that lies dormant in every living human being.

Intelligence-of-the-heart is purely a function of experienced innate consciousness.

The heart beats its rhythm, not because it is driven by a motor, but because it is itself the motor of blood circulation. Each cell of the heart beats this rhythm, and Dr. Carrel's experiment demonstrated what was well known to ancient wisdom concerning innate intelligence and consciousness. Each organic being (and even each cell of the organs of an organized being) has its part in the general life which is its personal specification. Man's heart is not alone in beating rhythmically like a motor: there are aquatic beings that are entirely a heart of this kind and represent *the awakening of the consciousness which will become "heart."* Another consciousness will become liver, another will become lung, and thus each function has its organ. Compared with an apparently inert mineral, for example, such an organ is the incarnation of a consciousness, of a cosmic function which has received corporeal life. A museum accordingly classifying "The Evolution of Consciousness" or "The Becoming of Life" as natural history would be much more authentic than our displays of dead specimens.

Every natural object in the universe is a hieroglyph of divine science. Each animal, each species of plant, each mineral group, is a stage in the process of "becoming aware" of the cosmic Cause, culminating in the complete organism of human man, the microcosm*— "man in His image."

The whole, thus formed into a complete living being, is a language that speaks. It expresses itself ceaselessly in its living function, and represents the basis of intelligence-of-the-heart, which is *the fact* that remains related to all of Nature and consequently *knows* Nature.

Knowledge of this kind cannot be objectified, but it is real. Reality is a fusion of consciousness with the object: there is identity. It is function experienced all by itself and innate in the organism which constitutes intelligence-of-the-heart. Obviously, therefore, we must be able to transcribe what is in us into our mental and objective consciousness, by establishing a relationship between the life in us and observation of that life in Nature. This we find supremely well expressed by the ancient Egyptians. It is a knowledge of magic, pure and sane, which can lead rapidly toward the spiritual goal of our lives, owing to the fact that we can evoke, by means of *the sympathy of analogues* in our surroundings, the consciousness of the heart latent in us.

---

*The "microcosm" is an image that makes it possible to perceive the idea being developed here. In reality, *man is the universe,* and not a miniature universe in the image of a large one.

Fundamentally, consciousness has two aspects: one is the result of comparisons, the other of identification. Both aspects need to be inscribed: one is an organic or cerebral inscription, the other is vital or functional.

It would be absurd to expect an identical functioning for cerebral consciousness and innate consciousness. The meaning of the term "consciousness" must be outlined and defined. We lack a suitable vocabulary for this meaning as we find it established in the ancient Egyptian and Hindu languages by masters of wisdom.

So let us say that cerebral consciousness is the result of quantitative experience, a mechanical consciousness resulting from comparison. Memory in itself is no more than a phonograph record or cinematographic film. A single impression is no more than an isolated groove of this record or one frame of this film. Functional memory, the definition of an impression recorded in this fashion, begins only with comparison. Even mechanically, one has to resort to "magic," that is, to *giving an impulse by evoking impressions.* For example, a particular flash of lightning evokes an entire scene from the past. A scent recalls an impression experienced long ago; a word ignites remembrance of a thought heard or read, and may give rise to a long series of "thoughts," of concordances. A fact recorded by the senses is what triggers recollection, and agreement or disagreement results in logical or illogical thought or sophistry. The entire cerebral mechanism can be reproduced mechanically. So much the better, as this will show the most obtuse of us where the error lies. But when we want to go beyond academic know-how — that sclerosis of the spirit — to fertile thought, the cerebral mechanism is no longer adequate. When we just said that we must necessarily turn to what constitutes true magic, namely, *evocation*, and that there is agreement or disagreement in the assemblage of recalled ideas, we were appealing to another power in us which comes from our innate consciousness, the source of the sense of harmony. If it is effective, this power will be the reason for genius, for creative thought, creative in the sense that it works ahead of the known, the classified.

Isn't it this consciousness of a new way, dictated to today's decadent world, which impels artists to destroy the idols of yesterday in order to attempt irrational expressions?

They seek a concordance of the elements of "sensations," ignoring the rational combinations which only satisfy the inertia of acquired habit. Atmospheres, images, and forms are created to evoke a feeling, an emotion, to provoke a vital reaction. Art is the herald of the mentality of a period, the harbinger of its innermost tendency.

Intelligence-of-the-heart, which establishes the relationship between innate consciousness and observation of fact, is identification.

Identification means to live with and to live in the observed fact, to be that fact oneself, to suffer it, to act in it, rejoice with it. It is sympathetic consciousness, not a subjective consciousness such as logic would like to oppose to objective consciousness. Yet confusion between the two is easy: cerebral consciousness is graphically inscribed in the cerebral matter, as we have just stated. Innate consciousness is inscribed in the nature of the organism, meaning that the motive power of its function is the impulse of its necessity, the Idea, or principle of harmony. In man, as already in the higher animal, this creates *emotivity*.

The greater the sensitivity of the emotional faculty, the better innate consciousness can express itself. If, then, the observed fact provokes a sensation, an emotional reaction of an egocentric order, this will be subjective consciousness. If the fact is observed by an individual in a state of neutrality, an impersonal state, this will be sympathetic consciousness. All these problems thus have their solution in the cultivation of self, in detachment from egoism, in the mastery of thought, of mentation, the cerebral cinema.

The inscription of innate or sympathetic consciousness is vital or functional, if life as such and function as such are considered the very principle of living Nature. This principle is a reality beyond corporeal matter, but it assumes a body; it incarnates by means of the harmony of the ambient elements.

When a certain number of elements exist, their relationship brings one or another function into play. For example, the earth breathes, the crab emerges from the sea, a plant germinates, the male palm tree grows toward the female palm tree .... Function is a necessity, and the latter pertains to the living law or genesis whose order effectuates the entire play of Nature, inborn knowledge of which is sacred science. Everything, absolutely everything, obeys this divine mandate, which is a simple set of functions imposed on the universe. And no intelligence can resist it, no power can hinder it; it is order, the harmony of the causal Cause working through the cosmic Cause.

The incarnation in man of all the necessities or functional orders of world harmony is the temple, where the original creative energy connects the intelligence-of-the-heart's innate consciousness with the universe. This comes about through objective observation of fact, in order to arrive at a cosmic consciousness independent of destructible or mortal components.

The science of this conscious return to the source (Christ arisen returns to the right of his Father, not into his Father) is spiritual psychology, and it speaks to us in this life, through Life.

Everything that lives, moves. This movement is either quantitative in space and time, or qualitative or formal; that is, it defines space and time. Force, in this case, is considered as Idea prior to formed substance or matter. Thus there is apparent life and the life which causes what is apparent.

Many attempts have been made to define life, but the only perfect definition would be that of life as divine Presence.

The term "dead body" is applied to a mineral, a dead plant, an inert animal that neither moves nor breathes, incapable of assimilating food, of experiencing an outer action, of expressing a feeling, a thought — in short, a cessation of the conscious relationship of the being with the environment. But anesthesia or catalepsy brings about all this to some extent, as does deep natural sleep.

Actually, a body is not dead until it decomposes into its constituent elements.

Thus, after cerebral consciousness has disappeared, there is still a possible vital subconsciousness within apparent death, and an innate life of matter after suppression of the subconsciousness. Consequently, there is a continuation of "dying" during bodily decomposition.

In fact, it is impossible to kill a being *born within Nature,* be it mineral or man.

Life is immanent in everything, from the indestructible fixed salt of the bones to complex consciousness.

For once, Lavoisier was correct, but not in the sense he intended, for if nothing can be lost, that which cannot be lost is always the same and unique thing, and everything, ultimately, is reduced to that same and unique thing.

We must speak about death in order to understand life. Definitive death does not exist; there are only changes of nonpermanent states. Permanence resides in the original Cause; the transitory is in the phases of self-awareness. The impulse toward this universal genesis is the life which causes what is apparent.

If definitive death does not exist (and this refers only to the natural being and not to *animated* man), it is because everything is life, whether this life has bodily form or whether it be metaphysical or form without body; that is, the Idea of the form becomes embodied. In the same way, the energetic lines of force of a "mother solution" are necessary to the crystal or assemblage of dispersed molecules. But there is also the ovum from which the fetus is generated. This no longer pertains to an assemblage of molecules dispersed in a solution: it is the corporeal formation of energy-elements selected by the

Idea within the nutritive medium. *The seed or paternal impulse is the Idea.*

Spirit, the divine Cause, is much closer to us than our poor brains can imagine.

Is the seed anything but the metaphysical Idea of the corporeal form it is going to generate? Is a catalyst anything other than the energetic Idea of the compound it brings about?

If the esoteric teaching of sacred science did not make it possible to prove that spirit is a fact, or to demonstrate what occurs in consciousness and in the successive phases of the "dying" of the body and of the transitory form, then all this teaching would be but gratuitous philosophical speculation devoid of value.

We say "God" and do not know what this means; we say "spirit" and do not understand this abstraction; we say "energy" and know nothing whatsoever of its nature.

We see effects and attribute to them a cause which is sometimes God, sometimes Spirit-Word, and sometimes Energy — words which take the place of ignorance but posit hypotheses we cannot avoid formulating.

Mere speculation cannot resolve these problems. It can only collect concrete, material elements perceived by the senses. Metaphysics makes no sense to the mind's reasoning.

On the other hand, once abstraction is hypothesized as a premise, we must seek the solution by the means at our disposal. These means are simply the teaching of Nature — of which we are the ultimate product — and our natural communion with her. When we want to express our knowledge, we must be able to translate or reduce it to concrete terms, accessible to our senses and rational through the cerebral function. "Sympathetic" experience always remains uncertain and open to discussion as long as it is not "objectified" experience.

Thus, to be as certain of our innate knowledge as we are of our learned knowledge, we must search for the experimental proof demonstrating that spirit, the abstract, actually becomes concrete by a definite route.

Sacred science affirms that this is possible. It teaches this through its "esoterism," which is "hermetically" sealed only from cerebral intelligence, and which will remain so unless we cultivate another aspect of intelligence and a mentality other than those sweepings off the granary floor which are our schools.

This is why the sages leave speculation to the idle, and contemplate Nature. Nature teaches everything. A sound evokes all its harmonics; an acorn evokes the oak — a harmonic complex which, in the plant kingdom, is oak. But musical harmonics are bodily vibrations of aquatic nature. The seed (sound or acorn, grain or spermatozoon) is of a specified nature, and this specification is the genesis of seeds from mineral to man, the *spatial reduction* of substance without form.

There is no "first seed," and the egg preceded the chicken. The substance of this egg has always existed as substance without form, the Cosmic Virgin. The sperm of the rooster, to the contrary, *became*, generated in the passage from cosmic nebula to itself.

The Christic principle, on the other hand, is direct fertilization without specific seed, a leap from the abstract origin to the ultimate human product: Man-God.

Appearance is the dualization of a single principle and defines Nature, or living spirit. The causal Cause is incomprehensible Unity and, metaphysically, from one becomes two, which results in the cosmic Cause, threefold in one Unity, the latter thus being accessible.

It is beyond our power to imagine anything that would not be possible in fact; that is, imagination (or any compilation of ideas) can only be composed of simple elements which are cerebrally accessible. Thus materialist philosophy, when it is logically consistent, has a real basis in Nature. But one unknown fact will mean an error in logic. It may be said: everything has always existed, and the varieties are the object of an evolution. This statement is both true and false. It is false if considered by bodily senses and cerebral intelligence alone; it is true spiritually because spirit, or substance without form, is eternal. It is that from which every body is formed. Evolution also is real, starting from the original energetic impulse, but it obeys a "law of universal genesis" and not fortuitous conditions.

Surely the function does not create the organ. How could it act before existing? Adaptation is not creation, and what is not created—that is, *contained in the harmonic order of the Law of Genesis*—will never be incarnated.

As for the evolutionist theory of materialism, it is bankrupt for most thinkers.

Besides, what is the good of philosophizing as our world has done for so many centuries? All our "philosophies" are but personal speculation compared with natural philosphy, the philosophy of living Nature and its summary as it is found in all sacred texts.

In the beginning, there is separation: this we still see always and everywhere. We need the number Two in order to define the number One, which, as indivisible Unity, is impossible for us to understand. The grain decomposes in the earth, the seed in the ovule. When we can no longer divide, we are beyond Nature and approach the causal Cause, the abstract Cause.

This is why the whole of metaphysics, all *creation*, is situated between the numbers One and Two. Then the threefold idea forms an accessible Unity which can be divided and added. The Chinese sages said: One always equals three. The Egyptian sages placed the triad at the origin of each line, as they placed the triangle at the origin of geometric forms. Two irreducible magnitudes are necessary to determine a third. The sages have never taught otherwise.

Becoming, or formation of substance into matter, is the mystery of reflection, that is, the phenomenon which is re-action. Neither action nor its reflector (the passive element of its nature) is a phenomenon. It is the reaction which is the effect of duality, and thus relative appearance.

And this is how the sacred Triad has formed Nature, the world, the universe.

We must look at this becoming as though we had been present at the *Fiat Lux* at beginning of time, with the certainty of actual eyewitness experience. Nothing prevents us from so doing, for time exists only for our physical senses, and the beginning of time is always present: were it not so, nothing would be maintained. Melchizedek-Osiris makes constant sacrifice.

We see activity by its effect. In its absolute, the active principle escapes us. The interplanetary or stellar world is black, complete darkness, in appearance. Should a body pass through, it will be luminous, lighted by ... the sun? Perhaps, but it will be lighted because this space of darkness is in reality wholly light. Absolute activity is unique; it is causal Cause and not cosmic Cause; it is Unity and not yet Three in One.

There must be an obstacle to measure the activity, to limit it, give it a value, a Number, so that it becomes *natural*. This already implies Two, that is, activity and obstacle.

"It is not good that the man should be alone; I will make him an help meet for him."

Nature, the universe, is nothing but the measure of the unknowable One—eternal God, the Almighty—because everything is virtually in Him, in the Self. This Measure contains all the functions of measures, the innumerable fractions each of which is a creature of this universe. The Egyptian cubits beautifully teach us the profound knowledge of those masters of wisdom for whom schematism was synonymous with death.

The opposition or obstacle is in reality no more understandable than the activity. The body which passes through dark space is unknown to us. But it opposes this light which is dark to our eyes. How could it do so, were it not of the same nature as light? The void is not an obstacle, just as transparent glass, for example, is not obstacle to light.

The thing which opposes must be of the same nature as the activity, and of at least a *lesser activity.* This subtraction is precisely the field of varieties. Subtraction, however, becomes division in a homogeneous medium. Let us suppose, for example, that milk is a perfectly homogeneous medium. When the fatty substance *rises* as cream on the milk, the homogeneity is destroyed.

There will be, finally, a watery whey and butter. Division has taken place, the active has manifested through opposition. In this instance, the active was a state of energy which is called *acid*.

This acid may be understood as *provoking the separation* of the homogeneous medium into water and fat; but from the first intimate separation, there will be the active and the obstacle, because the acid energy will have acted, finding in this medium the possibility of acting, that is, two separable things. Thus the components of the liquid milk are revealed, each with a very definite character, and even though they come from the same thing, they will no longer be at all in agreement. This crude example will serve to illustrate what we want to say.

We do not know what energy is, but it manifests itself as activity in various aspects, according to the medium. In the above example, it is acid, and everything complementary to this acid is alkaline. After separation, we find acid water and an alkaline fat, if it is fully separated and pure. However, in this imperfect world, acid and alkali always have a tendency to interchange. Here light is the acid; therefore what opposes it is alkaline, a lesser acid, and what is visible is fat, because it is separated from the water, that is, the light of the body illuminated in the darkness.

The light which we *see* is only *reaction*; the activating light is Cause; the obstacle, or the lesser reacting light, is the passive.

Adam knows himself in Eve; he recognizes the flesh and blood he was *without knowing it*. Before that, being identifed with his Cause, he possessed knowledge; now he has *learned to know*. These are the two intelligences of which the cerebral is the fall from the other—in the image of the Creator, but measured, limited.

This explanation might seem to be the esoterism of the words of Genesis. Yet it is no more than a simple explanation, a *cabala*, an exegis.

Esoterism is something quite different.

The entire universe, or phenomenal world, is dualized Unity, appearance—like reflected matter—or an activity against its own diminution or resistance.

The part of *lost activity* becomes the quantitative part of things, though absolute activity is not thereby diminished. For example, if we try to push a moving object which is itself moving at the same speed as we are, there will be no thrust. The difference in speed makes up the *quantity* of our effort. We cannot deny what is an *absurdum* for our mental intelligence, because this mystery of *Fiat Lux* is ceaselessly produced before us.

We can describe what takes place, we cannot say why it has happened, and thus we have to call upon another sense which will reveal to us the esoterism, that is, the *mystery*.

If we are then unable to describe this esoterism we have

known, we can at least consciously carry it out and put it into practice.

But there are several stages to be passed through in order to arrive at that.

The principle of *reaction* (reflection) is the *law of vital phenomena*. Everything that appears is the effect of reaction. Every organism lives only because of its faculty for reaction. Neither food nor medication can stimulate or heal without this reaction. Sound, light, all the effects of energy are reaction. Nothing can grow without reaction. Changes in the social order, whether natural or artificial, are reaction. Reaction is a modification of action in the sense of dualization. In the reaction, there is the child who stems from the father and mother, the life impulse and the substance which receives the impulse and produces the living body. And the day begins with the lunar night, reflected light, the substance in which the action of the active solar day can then continue. Could natural fire exist without fuell? fire without fuel is the causal Cause.

Thus to speak of Nature is to speak of duality, stability through equilibrium. But those who go higher are those who break through this stability, who know how to disunite in order to search the parts for what is eternal. Eternal equals eternal: then there is no more separation.

Pursuing the Absolute is as foolish as seeking security in mediocre stability, but to break up the latter without knowing how to deal with its parts is senseless destruction. To take away what is, to undo what is done, to destroy a composite and put the pieces together again, is all that free will can do: choice in the realm of quantity. It is negative. To generate bodies is a power of polarized spirit. Purification is a power of consciousness; it burns what is destructible in the parts in order finally to unify what was dualized.

9

*When classifying becoming into kingdoms, gene-
sis is time, matter or formed substance is space,
and activity (or form) is consciousness. Thus
Activity, Form, and Idea are different aspects of
the same puissance: the Self or cosmic consciousness which crystallizes—or is limited—in spatial
form, specific or qualified.*

Time is the distance between the seed and its fruit, between the sperm and the birth of its product, between
the creative impulse and the universe. Genesis is time;
we situate the cosmic and terrestrial cycles in its phases.
There is concordance, because the Law of Genesis is
identical for each thing. Duration is relative, like the
diameters of concentric circles, cycle within cycle. Thus
time in itself has no magnitude; there is only a difference of nature which situates within the kingdoms,
that is, a difference of specification.

The becoming of metaphysical or energetic substance
into physical matter or body is a spatial definition, the
limitation which makes space. This is Number. Thus
*space is not that in which a body is situated, but the body
itself*, whereas the medium in which it exists is the
abstract, metaphysical, energetic substance, that *corporeal nothingness* of which the world is made, that
Nothingness which is All. Cerebral intelligence,

corporeal and sensorial by nature, understands no other basis than the body, while it considers the noncorporeal as the container, or space. In reality, space is the All, the constant and absolute plenum. The body is a transient limit and becomes, by its limitation, perceptible to the senses. Number is but a fraction of Unity. Activity or Idea or Form is seed in general. In Nature, a particular seed is reduced activity or resistance, primary reaction, new activity. It could be described as a concentrated portion of space or void, acting on this void as in its passive medium. This is no vain speculation if we deepen our experimental study in order to see what, in the end, nourishes everything. There is a transition between this abstract substance and the concrete seed, but there is a thread easily followed in order to know it. We can cite here the fact of the activity of electrical energy in the vacuum of Crookes tubes: in this still relative vacuum, polarized energy produces all those phenomena which have led science to the atom.

The particularization of activity into seed is a stage in the becoming of consciousness, which begins with the *prima materia* of all things.

Between the numbers One and Two, the Self becomes the I, the Ego, the mathematical definition of the value One, as something in relation to itself. Next, with the *materia prima*—or original I—the becoming of consciousness finally begins to blend into the Self, once all experience has been acquired.

We must therefore use two different methods of thinking, and refuse to believe that one method alone can suffice, simply by changing the vocabulary, to clarify problems so diverse in nature. As stated earlier, this would lead straight to the formulation of nonsense.

10

There are two possible functions of logic, one cere-bral or mechanical, the other vital. The mechani-cal or syllogistic logic of quantity results from a comparison of concrete or definite elements. Vital logic is the logic of genesis or generation of a material form: it is the crystallization by time of the abstract Cause into spatial concrete form. The method of mechanical or cerebral logic is analy-tical. Vital logic requires the faculty of synthesis as spatial vision.

It seems folly to admit that there is any logic other than the classical syllogism. How can one arrive at a con-clusion when the given elements are abstract? Obvi-ously, this is only possible if an immutable law governs Becoming. The great though unrecognized merit of Hermetism was to formulate this law. Because of the obsession with "alchemy," the mirage of gold, the philosophy of Hermetism has been neglected. Yet there is no difference between this formulation and the pronouncement of the Mosaic Genesis which, in its essence, we encounter in all sacred texts.

In the process of generation, which demands an active impulse in a medium homogeneous with this activity (as a seed in the earth is moistened by the water which fed the seed), there is always, before all else, decomposition (putrefaction) of this material into a chaotic, mucilaginous form. The second phase is the formation of a new center of attraction (nucleus, cell) which draws nutritive substance to it. This substance, in turn, constantly undergoes the same decomposition, which creates the succession of death (decomposition) and of life (reconstruction) for re-generating substance and producing growth. Thus, in decomposition, there appears a part which is *Earth*, meaning fixed, and another part which is *Water*, that is, volatile or nutritive. In a plant, one is the root, the other the germ; in the cell, one is the nucleus and the other cytoplasm. As for growth, it is limited by the *active Fire* of the seed, its assimilative power.

This, roughly speaking, is the mechanism of Becoming, beginning from a specific seed, and this function is repeated, without stopping, up to the formation of the new seed. What makes the "mystery" here is the nature of the nutritive substance. In fact, if everything on earth merely grew out of existing chemical elements, growth would be no more than the constant migration of these simple elements from one complex form to another, after reduction to their simple nature. But, visibly, the earth increases, humus is accumulated with the dust of our ancestors' bones. After billions of years, all the water of the oceans would not suffice to make the rain which nourishes terrestrial vegetation. To assume a constant circulation of these same waters is an over-simplification. At intervals, the waters enter into all the materials that raise the level of the surface, covering over past civilizations, forming geological strata. The earth lives like everything else in the universe, meaning that spirit is reduced to space, or to things which return to that spirit after completing the cycle: first, corporeal genesis; then, the cycle of the genesis of consciousness.

It is characteristic of sacred texts that they develop each genesis in full detail, with every nuance of meaning, as a gnosis for those whose "hearts are open."

It is necessary to understand the reality of volume, and this is absolutely impossible to grasp cerebrally. We know that it exists, since our senses stem from it, but we always have to slice this volume in order to understand it. We understand addition and subtraction, since these concern quantity, but multiplication and division — that is, extension in volume and its decomposition into spatial components—are beyond our grasp.

In the corporeal genesis described above, the meaning of decomposition by putrefaction completely escapes us. Corruption, namely, chemical displacement, is familiar to us, but "creative" putrefaction has nothing in common with it. The hen's egg putrefies in order to "create" the living germ, but corruption, to the contrary, destroys. Living putrefaction gives rise to new elements which, chemically speaking, did not previously exist. There is much more hydrogen sulfide in a rotten egg than the traces of sulphur in a fresh egg could produce. The mysterious albumin and albuminoid substances are products of this genesis of life.

All attempts to describe this life are useless and will always deceive, just as it is impossible to explain how a point becomes a surface, how One becomes Two. The

Euclidian *exoteric* theory is practical but absurd. It was employed in ancient Egypt for ordinary purposes, but sacred geometry began from volume and not from "a point which results from the intersection of two lines which themselves come from the movement of the point." The whole of materialist, rationalist philosophy is based on the absurd, and necessarily so, while esoteric philosophy, or sacred science, is *based on fact* in order to know Cause. Everything is space, which means that it has volume. There is no point, in the sense of one sole-singular comprehensible moment in the universe. The sliced volume gives the planes, the angles of the lines of intersection give the point which, in the simplest case, is the result of the meeting of three lines of intersection. The point is ternary. The cosmic Cause is ternary; every comprehensible beginning is "three in one." Everything resulting from this is comprehensible, and constitutes rational science. The error of our science is to want to penetrate the mysteries of life through its ordinary means of comprehension.

To recognize the point which results from volume instead of following Euclid's proposition would be to adopt a wholly new attitude, accepting *a priori* the existence of a metaphysical world. (This would be wisdom, but we prefer the absurd because it is practical.)

It would be to search for vital logic, for a science of life that looks upon the interstellar "void" as Fire, the nutritive substance whence come all things owing to the cycle of a genesis conforming to immutable Law.

But we are absolutely determined to understand

through the logic of the mind, and flashes of intelligence, such as that which conceived of entropy, come to naught because of this desire to explain in concrete terms.

This substance, which is the "void," is neither hot nor cold as long as it is not in movement. To increase volume mechanically means allowing it to absorb this void, and to contract volume is to liberate the void: hence the effect of heat and cold. To generate a material form is to fix the void, and nothing in the world is more fixed than this "void."

What cannot be burned is the void fixed to a degree equal to the heat which acts upon it. There is a chemistry and a physics of "vital logic."

From putrefying flesh, primitive animal life is born; but since this is not understood, it is said that there existed seed, spores, and eggs.

Syllogism is mechanical logic and can only resolve mechanical problems, that is, relations of quantities. Its method is analytical because only the decomposition of a composite into its elements makes it possible to understand, that is, to know and to define what composes it. By this route, we soon come to irreducible elements where analysis confronts the boundary wall of cerebral intelligence, the mental faculty. This is the frontier of the earthly Paradise, guarded by an angel with a flaming sword, in the East where the eye of God, the Sun, rises.

There is no way back into this garden of "fused identity" because there is no inside and outside to it: only those who have come out of it have *learned to know* this distinction, and to "come out" means to divide.

It is necessary to relearn this vision of the One who is "within the thing"; who decays, grows, expands, lives, fructifies, and dies with it, in it.

On the plane, twice two makes four, and twice four makes the *cube* of two, all this by addition and movement of the plane. But it takes twenty-seven cubes for the original cube to grow, doubling itself in all directions in space. One may add cubes to cubes, but one must be able to be cube with the cube in order to know it. This is the faculty of *synthesis*. We are advised as a discipline of thought to objectify every idea. The sage, to the contrary, seeks to put an end to duality. One *learns to know* the object, but one *knows* life through inborn knowledge.

11

The definition of anything whatsoever in the natural or physical universe is innate consciousness. Essentially, this inborn consciousness, in its final fulfillment, is, for the mineral: affinity; for the plant: affinity, growth, and generation of fruit or seed; for the animal: affinity, growth, free movement, and cerebral intelligence, which bestows instinct. For the human-animal, all the preceding consciousnesses are innate, and reason develops, which will make man conscious of consciousness. Here begins the capacity for liberation from material form, the return, after all the natural consciousnesses have been realized.

The term "consciousness" is used philosophically in different ways, but always and of necessity includes a relationship between two elements and the faculty of memory. Understood in this way, consciousness of fused identity would be nonsensical.

But we can also define consciousness as being that specific quality of a thing endowing it with the capacity to select by affinity, which is then a true "remembering" of its position in relation to other things. For example, a molecule of a simple chemical body has very precise affinities toward other molecules and makes the choice for its alliance according to surrounding conditions.

There is no free will for the mineral; it is governed by *predetermined necessity.* In man's cerebral life, "affinities," or associations of ideas, can vary, yet the fundamental function remains the same as that of the chemical affinity of bodies. Character, the qualitative definition of things, is man's innate consciousness of things, without regard for the circumstances forming this character.

One can always find a physical explanation for every phenomenon, even for the tendril of a plant unerringly reaching out for support across empty space. Is this due to magnetism? Or because of infrared or some other radiation? It doesn't matter: the plant, like the mineral,* is alive, and this tendency of the tendril (and not of any other part of the plant) to find a way to attach itself is an aspect of plant consciousness, whose purpose, in general, is to feed itself *selectively* through affinity, to grow and to produce fruit, which is seed.

To complete this idea, we should here note the seminal nature of the mineral, according to Hermetic science.

---

* With increasing frequency, one encounters very authoritative articles concerning the necessity of seeking a better mode of spiritual life, propounding a psychological philosophy based on the teachings of all times. It is strange to encounter complete silence in these writings with regard to the life of the mineral, which is, nevertheless, the foundation of all earthly life. Here something is missing — perhaps intentionally so—but which therefore should at least be mentioned, unless it is simply a matter of ignorance.

The center, so to speak, of the mineral kingdom is the metal. Premetallic and postmetallic substances should be classified as metalloids. The latter reach into the plant kingdom and are found in the animal kingdom as well. Metal is thus the mineral trunk which will bear the fruit. This fruit or seed is metal itself, that is, there is a successive elimination of every substance which is not seed. Thus there are two seeds or fruits, just as there is a seven-month embryonic child and a nine-month embryonic child. The first is Silver, white in nature and of feminine character; the second is Gold. These characteristics are not to be considered as referring to sexualized types, but each includes in itself its complement and is the two sexes reunited in one Unity. The feminine Silver contains the fixed male nature, and Gold is wholly Silver, animated by male Fire. Silver, that "Queen of Peace," can never play the feminine role for Gold. Gold in the metallic realm typically parallels the universal Christic principle. It is the *natural* perfection of the original intention, and thus becomes the foundation stone for the return to the Source.

Therefore, a multiplicity of metallic individualities does not exist. There is only a single metallic state which generates metallic seed: of the white nature, into Silver; of the red nature, into Gold: comparable to a plant with roots in premetallic matter producing seed, trunk, branch, leaf, and flower—all apparently distinct "metals" —in order to bear these two seeds. The essences, resins, sap, and exhalations of this metallic plant produce postmetallic substances.

This doctrine perfectly conforms to the universal

religious cosmogony, and the analogies lend precision to the esoteric meaning. From this springs a real knowledge of the entire psychospiritual science concerned with the generation of consciousness. It is to this latter lineage that Buddhism should be related. It would be absolutely incorrect to consider the Buddha and Christ as identical.

Christ is to be seen as Gold, the incarnation of the divine Word, Man-God and God-Man: the divine in Nature.

To this principle is related the sense of redemption, which does not appertain to the Buddha. But this does not mean there is a hierarchy of values of the divine Word. Both the Buddhist and Christic ways are expressions of truth; however, we must distinguish between the ways that are taught. Christ, like the Buddha, is in all men, just as the seed in the premetallic is metal. It is a matter of bringing this seed to maturity.

If the Law of Genesis is unique and universal and gives rise to analogies, it is nevertheless manifested at different stages of the overall genesis. It can therefore be applied, on the one hand, to the genesis of every plant, from root to flower-fruit, as in psychospiritual practices, especially the Buddhist and Brahmanic, which *progressively* eliminate heterogeneities in order to produce the pure Lotus in its seed. On the other hand, there is the Way of Redemption, which eliminates every impurity *at one stroke,* and acts only on the substance restored to its originality (the Cosmic Virgin), and produces this fruit—*bypassing Nature* and dualization. This starts from the principle that the divine *intention* is perfection, consciousness of the Self, earthly Paradise, and conscious Unity, while dualization, or "original sin," has produced this imperfect, suffering Nature. Accordingly, these are two aspects of one and the same sacerdotal science: Osiris and Horus.

In order to understand the mystery of the highest teaching given to man, we must first know the instrument offered to us, after the innumerable series of sufferings which have gone before and comprise our present life.

For suffering is the only stylus whose nature corresponds to the substance on which imperishable consciousness is inscribed. The stone has suffered for the plant, the plant has suffered for the animal, the animal has suffered for man, and man has suffered for Redemption.

And those who have gone further than we have, they are the Powers and the Masters who stretch out their hands to help us, as the sea stirs the desire of the sailor for the offing, or the summit challenges the daring of the mountain climber.

The expanding warmth of the heart, when it reveals as rational what is generally considered irrational, when it allows us surefootedly to cross this gulf, which we can then ignore, and which terrifies the others: this warmth is the call of the Master.

Tendency is tension, affinity is love, appetite is need, but we must say with the Proverb: "I know not the way of a man with a maid" (Prov. 30: 18-19).

The experience of life inscribed in matter is called *innate consciousness*, the specific character of each thing, the quality that is pure spirit in Nature.

The animal is a freely moving plant because all the phases of its gestation are fixed in organs — that is to say, in specific individualizations — and because the root has become intestine, the leaf has become lung, the taproot has become stomach, the circulation of sap has become blood and veins, and the flower has become sex. This totality has been linked together by the marrow to form a conductive organ, the brain, and through that has become cerebral intelligence, which is conscious memory, and makes possible the expression of the innate consciousness that creates instinct. The faculty of coordinating ideas is still lacking in order for man to exist.

When one beholds the emotional reactions of the animal—envy, hate, fidelity, love, joy, sadness, devotion to his master to the point of self-denial — one says that an animal sometimes seems human. This is a mistake: it is man who is still an animal. All emotional reactions are based on egoism, the first cerebral consciousness of oneself, a mirror of the object, a freed slave. From a moral point of view, these emotional reactions are natural. But only man has in him that gift allowing him to free himself from all these reactions; to attain aristocratic liberty by fusing with the Whole—love without cause, without aim, without reward, and therefore without deception.

This gift is Reason, which makes Man out of the animal; this is the second birth into the world, for Nature stops at the animal, including the human animal. The baptism of the spirit, the Pentecost which gives Reason, is a second *Fiat Lux*.

Reason affirms in us what the brain cannot understand—*a priori* knowledge; Reason shows us the nobility of the useless which is beauty, pardon, faith, sacrifice: the sacred act.

Reason is the intelligence-of-the-heart which allows us, in love, to be the thing, to be inside the thing, to grow with the plant, to fly with the bird, to glide with the serpent, to be that "way of a man with a maid" which the Proverb says cannot be known; to become cubic space with the cube.

It is to this Reason that esoterism addresses itself.

But we have prostituted this Reason and made it into a utilitarian rationalism, the mentality of merchants for whom the scales are the working tool, for whom everything has its countervalue, its counterweight, leading to equational logic, the erudite decimal system, algebra.

But in life, each moment is different from the preceding, the genesis of the world never ceases, nor the turning of the spheres, the cycles: nothing ever returns to the same place. All in the universe is in interdependent connection with All.

12

The disaggregation of any being can affect its quantity through analysis or "mechanical logic," but starting with conscious man, it can affect his quality of self-consciousness. In principle, both roads lead to the same natural source, but the first is original and causal; the second is final and creative, conscious, beyond Nature. The first source is polarized and dependent energy, and thus destructive toward things; the second is non-polarized energy, independent of dualized Nature.

In Nature, everything is composite, an aggregate of quantities; yet energy—spirit—is not composite.

Outside Nature, originally and ultimately, spirit is non-polarized, but it is polarized in Nature. This is yet another way of stating the theme. Thus energy will *appear*, in its action upon things, in triple rather than double aspect, because the poles themselves appear only in their effects: North attracts and South repels; South against South repels; North and South complement one another, attract one another; North against North is neutral. These are the *three* aspects of energy. May the atomic wizards tolerate our incursion into their domain, but they have yet to understand Nature as made in the image of That, the Selfsame, God, and they have yet to perceive the reliable microscope of natural philosophy as superior to the electron microscope.

To decompose the material aggregation by force is to free its "void," that energy which will necessarily be immediately repolarized. Being freed arbitrarily, it remains linked to the natural thing and, like an octopus, will grab onto everything in its surroundings. But pertaining to the Origin, this energy can act even on the elements of permanence innate in the substance of beings.

On the other hand, this liberation may occur in the course of a natural genesis which always tends toward return to the original source and, by this route, reaches its aim while including *all the innate consciousnesses.* Then the original dualization comes to an end; multiplicity and variety are no longer required; the energy is no longer polarized and becomes beneficent Fire, conscious, creative, generating.

13

Innate consciousness is inscribed in matter and is subject to all its transformations, birth and death, while preserving its essential characteristics, which are transmitted.

Vital consciousness is inscribed in the immortal essence of material form, meaning that causal power, through the moment of awareness of all Nature, seeks the possibility of its reliberation or self-consciousness, beyond the material instrument.

Let us take an example from the following illustration. Directly or indirectly, solar radiation is what makes the plant. This radiation makes a pine tree or an ear of wheat. The radiation is impartial and universal, but through the seed it is specified as pine tree or wheat.

From this moment on, it is characterized by the particular innate consciousness of one of these plants.

When this same radiation returns to its source, after passing through its material form, it bears this innate consciousness. This is not possible for a particular consciousness which always brings back the radiation characterized by what is of the nature of pine tree or wheat: the universal in its return demands universality of experiences for a universal consciousness.

Since the radiation in itself is nonspecified, it is therefore in the generated seed that the characteristic is fixed,
and it is this which must undergo transformation in the
universal genesis.

Fixed in a material form, the seed is the part which
retains acquired consciousness. Conversely, we may
say: it is the indestructible and immutable fixed part of a
thing which represents the seed of continuations in the
cycle of cosmic genesis, and attracts to itself the next
radiation in order to make a new individual.* This
attraction by a specified fixed point necessarily makes a
selection from radiation, just as the leaves and colored
petals of a plant select luminous rays.

This selection constitutes the adaptation of the radiance
to the innate consciousness, be it of pine tree or of
wheat. Therefore, neither one nor the other is the total,
universal radiation, the evolutionary path toward that
universal consciousness which this particular seed must
pursue. Thus this genesis takes place in the fixity of
matter.

At the level of the human animal, all possibilities of the
evolution of material consciousness are exhausted. It
then becomes a question either of a physical continuity
(the legend of the Wandering Jew) or of a new baptism
of spirit, allowing the original radiance to reliberate
itself from matter, all experiences exhausted, meaning
no further selection is to be made in the materialization
of this radiance: it is received into its universality.

*This is the meaning of the Egyptian *ka*.

54

Physical continuity makes a selection, reliberation no longer does so. (The Apostles speak in all tongues after the descent of the Holy Spirit.)

It is a moment of grace.

This grace is offered to every living man: he need only utilize his acquired faculties in order to become receptive to it.

It is the inspired breath of the living soul, received by the father, Adam, and preserved in a state of sleep in his descendants.

This is where there may occur the only *death* possible: there exists the possibility of disintegration between the human being and the *living* soul. This death involves the conscious denial of that living soul, also known as the sin against the Holy Spirit, the most unpardonable of sins.

Awakening is the awakening of intelligence-of-the-heart. Reason is born with us. If we give it preponderance over cerebral intelligence, over the mental, it will tell us everything, for it is the intelligence of the universe.

The stages of this liberation are therefore stages of fusion. The inscription is no longer seminal; it is only a *degree of detachment*. Mastery of the body and all its members, mastery of thought, mastery of the passions, are only stages of a liberation which allows this soul, *as in natural sleep*, to live in full consciousness, without the material instrument, outside the definitive sleep of our present body.

To succeed in "sleeping" thus in a waking state is the true clairvoyance of intelligence-of-the-heart.*

* In *Journey Into the Light* (New York: Inner Traditions, 1984), Isha Schwaller de Lubicz defines various aspects of innate consciousness, and the twofold aspects of the immortal soul as "Human Consciousness," "Permanent Witness," and "Spiritual Witness."

14

The faculty of "hearing" instinct and translating it in the brain is intuition. This faculty of translating constitutes intelligence-of-the-heart.

Intelligence-of-the-heart is what enables man to make his way toward liberation. It is to intelligence-of-the-heart that the scripture or oral tradition of an esoteric teaching is addressed, and phrased in a manner most conformable to that faculty, even at the risk of seeming irrational.

If we are able to prevent the intervention of reasoning — that faculty distinguishing us from the animal properly so-called, and which we constantly abuse — then simple cerebral intelligence does no more than translate innate consciousness, as in the case of animal instinct.

Our senses suffice for the observation of instinctive effects. They are in touch with the four principial elements which are the constituents of Nature.

But to know innate consciousness, we must hearken to it, make use of the spiritual sense which is Hearing; similarly, the thumb serves as the finger of spirit in relation to the four (elemental) fingers of the hand.

This is difficult, if not impossible, to explain. *To hear* what is nothing other than a physical silence (the voice of silence) is the faculty that makes translation possible. It is intelligence-of-the-heart that appears as intuition, inherent knowledge of what the brain has not yet classified as learned knowledge.

In every life situation, we experience an emotion. This emotion must be *heard;* we have to *center* the hearing on the emotion in order to be conscious of our instinctive attitude toward the vital moment in question.

From that instant, we *know* what it means or, less subtly phrased, we have an intuition of the answer to the question which has arisen.

Intuition means *hearing* the voice of silence that speaks in all lived Nature, innate in us, with a *cosmic din.*

Intelligence-of-the-heart is knowing how to translate this noise.

Thus the purpose of initiatory texts is far less a logical one than it is to provoke shocks, emotional reactions, or to grate against the cerebral need for sequential logic. Paradox, improbable images, the juxtaposition of unconnected phrases are freely employed. The texts appeal to sensation, to a feeling of emotive sensitivity.

The truest expression, the fundamental expression, as it were, is provided by Number. The faculty of enumerating is *a priori* knowledge, innate consciousness of Nature: duality is relationship; it is counting. A molecule counts its affinities according to its valence. A plant seeks its support and grows upward: all discrimination is counting. An animal counts its young. But there are characteristic limits to the conscious state, to the experience inborn in each entity. The science of Number is not that of numerals, not even that of the proportions which constitute ordinary geometry. Search as we may for combinations and series, even with the renowned Golden Section, or Golden Mean, the esoterism of Numbers will never be revealed to us that way.*

Number is living, an expression of life, and speaks directly to intelligence-of-the-heart. Its true secret lies in the becoming of One into Two.

* We suggest that true lovers of the esoterism of the Golden Section should study ancient Egypt. Here *Phi* and all its applications, including the development of $6\phi^2/5$ which plays the role of Pi, are applied with a true knowledge of Number of which the West—even in the Renaissance—was unaware. Only the initiates of the great but brief "Gothic epoch" can be considered directly related to the Pharaonic sages.

15

Rational universe and metaphysical universe do not exist as essentially different entities, but there is spirit or threefold Word. Likewise, there is not energy and matter, there is spirit-substance and form. There is not microcosm and macrocosm, there is spirit and life. There are not two banks of a river, there is the earth and the river flowing on it whence comes earth, just as spirit—or substance— produces matter through the action of form.

Appearances are relative, therefore transient. Consciousness innate in matter is purely a sequence of the phases of spirit becoming conscious of itself in all the possibilities of its reflections. When no more reflections are possible, there is conscious immortality.

What a thing comes from is what it returns to. Yet no cycle in Nature closes at its exact starting point; otherwise Nature would be absolute, and there would be no becoming and no return. The return to the origin is therefore only absolute for the causal Cause. It is not an infinite cycle since the infinite, the irrational, is indefinite, whereas the return to the origin is precisely the cycle which defines Nature. Nothing, for us, is more definite than the absolute, irrational cycle, since this is what makes Nature, the perceptible universe, for which—in which—no cycle can be absolute.

We can never think without dividing in order to compare. The infinite is incomprehensible; consequently, we wish for what is definite. We are in the cycle of Nature, which is the circle of becoming and return. If we break it, the ring is a beginning and an end at every moment, and this break is what our cerebral intelligence demands.

Reason, on the other hand, can conceive of this ring and affirm it, just as it affirms the spherical spiral in the case of swelling a spherical volume, since radial development makes such expansion impossible. Yet, here again, we are only able to understand the plane spiral. Reason imposes the notion of an indivisible unity, and this is absurd to cerebral intelligence.

Reason proceeds by affirmation; it does not explain, since it is inborn knowledge, implicit in everything and in ourselves.

Man is a cosmos, *the cosmos*. There is nothing in the world which is not in him, either potentially or in actual fact. The material form of man is the eternal ring which, through birth and death, manifests the break. This break affects only the natural aspect; the circle always subsists: nothing is more fixed than the void, nothing more stable than the cycle of becoming and return, the absolute circle. Our sliding on this ring, which is the genesis of becoming and the genesis of return, gives us the illusion of movement, and attributes to this circle a magnitude through time.

The break causes reflection, reaction. An electric or magnetic circuit produces a phenomenon only by virtue of interruption. Everything represents an un-interrupted electric or magnetic circuit, since all rotation produces a magnetic axis and an electric equator, and since everything moves: corporeally in its atoms or molecules, vitally in the natural cycle. The broken circuit makes a going or positive pole, and a returning, relatively negative pole which is the reflection of the former. The cycle always tends to close up again since the ring in its essence is eternal, and the link joining the corporeal ends of the break is the phenomenon, the *appearance of the circuit*.

Thus man is an appearance in the moment, the site of the eternal ring now manifesting itself in the human being. It is nothing but a dialectic subterfuge to compare a microcosm with a macrocosm in order to show the celestial influence on sublunary things, things which endure it. For nothing can be subjected to any influence whatsoever if the subject is not of the same nature as the influence. A stick is powerless against spirit, idea speaks to idea, reason to reason, reasoning to the brain. The stellar universe has no influence on the earth, because the latter is identical in nature with the heavens, with their harmony and substance; and this identity of heaven and earth is the arcanum.

If there were a difference, man the microcosm would be

a lesser quantity than macrocosmic man. But size does not exist for pure quality. A dog is not a microcosm, it is an element, an organ, an aspect of it, not a part, but a transitory state of it. Man, to the contrary, is a totality and, for that reason, he himself is the cosmos. This wholeness in him is virtual; it becomes actual when his consciousness is liberated from mortal contingencies, is realized as intelligence-of-the-heart, free of all necessary comparisons; *consciousness in itself*, with no further reflection, hence without break: the closed ring, the entire cosmic phenomenon.

16

Everything in the universe represents one of the possibilities imminent in the Source or Word or threefold Logos. We could say "energy" as well. Thus each thing is the image or expression or writing of this possibility: medu-Neter *(in graphic form, the hieroglyphs). To transcribe consciousness, we can make use of image or hieroglyph, or else create a conventional script.*

Just as the tree is virtually, in ideal form, contained in the seed, so is the universe contained in the threefold Word of the omnipresent Origin. All the forms of seed are materialized in the Tree of the World, and each part is one of the *medu-Neter*, the sign writing or "runic wand," revealing the idea. In this way, we can read possibility, divine entity, through the manifestations of Nature: this is Egypt. Each is *deva, daimon, Neter*, as a general type. To express a function, the most perfect, complete, and truly irreplaceable esoteric writing is the pictorial representation of things, or even the synthesis of the characters of diverse things.

When these *medu-Neter* are eventually organized into a system, an alphabet, grammar, and syntax, hieroglyphic writing is the result. It moves away from the original perfection, but makes it possible to address the uninitiated also, with a minimum of error, cabalistically

instilling a possible meaning with a human corre-
spondence parallel to the primordial esoteric meaning.
The latter is understandable to the well-prepared reader
alone. The ordinary meaning is legible to everyone and
serves as an excellent guide, if one knows how to look
behind it specifically for the *medu-Neter.*

We prefer to use the Egyptian words *medu-Neter* when
speaking of esoteric writing in order to distinguish its
intention from that of the Hellenized word "hieroglyph," which refers to a completely organized and
exoteric writing.* But hieroglyphic figures are too often
wrongly considered to be symbols in the ordinary sense
of the term, and an error of interpretation is consequently so easily made as to be almost inevitable.

*For the deciphering of this writing, we remain profoundly indebted to
Champollion, a scholar of true genius.

17

The symbol is a conventional representation. The hieroglyph is direct, nonconventional writing, and only a hieroglyph is able directly to transcribe the intelligence-of-the-heart and be translated thereafter by the cerebral intelligence. Any other method of esoteric writing either requires the elimination of much of the grammatical form—leaving it to the reader to gather the meaning of the words without imposing a frame of reference—or else resorts to devices such as allegory, metaphor, parable, play on words, or phonetic cabalism.

In its original meaning, the word "symbol" is a synonym of "coincidence," or the complementation of two parts of a whole. In the broader sense, it has come to mean convention. In this latter meaning, it can no longer be applied to hieroglyphic signs. An image is not the conventional representation of an object; it evokes the object as represented by its typical features or essential characteristics. Used in this way, even color is not conventional for floral vegetation, for the latter is green, as are moss and mildew.

Each color thus responds to one phase of genesis, and is connected with the two principal lines of the whole of Nature, which the two crowns of Egypt represent. The strange forms of these crowns should draw attention to their real and not their conventional significance.

Pharaonic hieroglyphic writing in its essence is not conventional, as long as it is *medu-Neter*.

A degree of conventionality enters into organized exoteric writing, however, but the conventional choice is always made with great care in order not to stray too far from the esoteric meaning. Here below, nothing is absolute. Pictorial writing is the only means of conveying a thought directly to intelligence-of-the-heart. A child reads pictures without knowing the words that transcribe intelligently to others what he experiences. A child always tries to express himself through gestures or actions. He is much closer to the truth than the learned man, for whom words with fixed meanings are merely sounds lined up in a more or less pleasing manner. Alas for our literature!

The conventional ideogram is readable in all languages.*

Hieroglyphic writing cannot be read in this way. It demands to be read for what it expresses in particular and to be transcribed later—as best one can. This spoken language, like the writing, is based on gnosis. Each letter, each root, obeys a natural law, an exact, living law. No letter can be pronounced without setting into action specific nerve centers. Thus there is a vital reason for constructing their "alphabetical" sequence, and a definite law for relating them by roots.

Furthermore, in order to express themselves in alpha-

* In this connection, apart from a universal language, a United States of Europe will never come into being without a unifying ideographic writing.

betical languages composed of conventional signs, the sages have always employed subterfuge. The most perfect method, in this respect, is the one we find in the original sacred texts of India, and in the Books of Moses, before the introduction of mother vowels, and then of vocal points, to fix the sound of vague, unwritten vowels. Nouns, generally without connections between them, make a kind of telegraphic style of writing. The reader has to put the sense of these words together according to what he "hears" or "understands." Man will always be led astray by the logical meaning of an idea, in the same way that he will be much more attracted by a recipe than by philosophy. What is immediate is easy, what is useful easily attracts us, but to think is irksome; the useless irritates the lazy person. Idleness and inertia rule the whole of Nature, which, in the absence of a new impulse of energy, degenerates, goes the way of least resistance, breaks up, is degraded, and falls. This applies to all things.

Therefore, if we see generation of a life, it means that something new has been introduced.

The literary parable is like the geometric parabola: a focus in the center and innumerable parallel rays concentrated there by reflection. Allegory, on the other hand, turns around the center like a cat around a plate that is too hot. Allegory is misleading or even childish when it tries to be sincere. Metaphor is a trick unworthy of esoterism. Play on words calls for much erudition and etymological knowledge. This means is the most akin to the Kabbalah. It can be constructed on phonetic relationship.

18

The Kabbalah, as revelation of the esoteric meaning of the Testament of Moses, has given rise to a very false notion of esoterism. The Genesis of Moses includes an esoterism, but it is written in a historical style which is satisfying to ordinary intelligence and is also found in the evangelical key: the Passion. The Kabbalah, on the other hand, speaks of the metaphysical history of this Genesis, as does the Apocalypse in the Gospels. There is a parallelism in these two modes of revelation, even though they are basically very different.

Neither the Kabbalah nor the Apocalypse is an explanation of the esoterism of the principal text, but another aspect of this text. Esoterism does not explain itself and cannot be spelled out: it concerns the consciousness of the disciple and not a doctrine.

Cabala, or revelation, has become synonymous with mystery and intrigue. Returning to the real meaning of this term, we find there is also an Egyptian, a Buddhist, and a Christian cabala.

The Egyptian cabala includes the Pyramid Texts and what is called the history of the *Dwat, The Book of the Dead.*

It is the recital of the soul: an analysis of dissociation and affinities, of the aim of the endeavor to retain the soul, of the maleficent or beneficent consequences of the acts of the living.

This is truly psychospiritual science. In Egypt, it takes on the character of complete knowledge, based on a priestly science. In Buddhism, because of the absence of a fundamental myth, it assumes a more literary character.

There is a close kinship between the Pharaonic and the Brahmanic cabala.

The Hebrew Kabbalah, revelation of the Mosaic teaching, comes from Egypt and retains a kinship with this origin, although modified by the nature of the Jewish mission and by several Commentaries.

Each of the Pyramid Texts is complete in itself. They are superimposed to convey different shades of meaning for certain passages, the key to such modifications being given by the meaning of the King's name.

As for the Christian cabala, considered in this context, it has experienced what happens to people who live together all the time: from seeing each other so often, they no longer know one another. It will always seem more attractive and romantic to speak of a Master in India than of a Western saint. The astral world arouses much more curiosity than a study of Purgatory, and so on.

In fact, the asexual character of the Christian myth has colored its entire teaching with a sort of sexual inhibition which places the Christian cabala apart from the contingencies of life here below. Further, its purely moral character smothers the basis of gnosis, which is as complete here as elsewhere.

This is in striking contrast to the Atlantean black cabala, based entirely on sex, that is to say, on the sexualization or dualization of the causal Cause, God sole-singular and Unknowable. It is tempting, especially in the Christian world, to label this theology black magic, the magic of evil, which is as inane as condemning our parents to hell for having conceived us in sin. If the first Christians had followed Saint Paul's counsels of chastity, no one would have remained to propagate the new faith.

The seeker after God should look at His Work; it is the Book one must learn to read by breaking the seven seals. Evil is at the origin, in consciousness, when knowledge becomes know-how, and intelligence-of-the-heart falls into "the devil's laboratory," into this brain, imitator of the creative Work.

There is much more real evil in our *rational* science than in the sexual rites of the great African forest.

A cabala is not the esoterism of sacred texts. It is the history of the soul's consciousness. History is succession in time. Esoterism is intelligence-of-the-heart, spatial vision, fused identity, ouside of time, ex-stasis.

73

19

Esoterism is not a particular meaning hidden in a text, but a state of fusion between the vital state of the reader and the vital state of the author: this in the sense of a spiritual, spatial, synthetic vision which disappears at precisely the moment thought becomes concrete.

Thus esoteric teaching is strictly evocation, and can be nothing other than that. Initiation does not reside in any text whatsoever, but in the cultivation of intelligence-of-the-heart. Then there is no longer anything occult or secret, because the intention of the enlightened, the prophets, and the "messengers from above" is never to conceal—quite the contrary.

This last statement needs no further commentary. Everything these simple remarks could contain has already been said.

May the people of our time, who by reason of the alleged comforts derived from their scientific technology are falling more and more deeply into matter, come to understand that if the end of bodily life is death, the end of what constitutes the body's life is to survive and liberate itself from what is mortal.

The means of attaining this end is no more difficult than it is to *live*. Yet this is precisely what few people know how to do. Most are solely concerned with distracting themselves, passing the time that separates them from the hour of the death they so greatly fear.

To live is not to work. If we are condemned to work in order to maintain our life, this sentence constitutes the suffering through which we must acquire the intelligence-of-the-heart that is, in itself, our life's spiritual aim.

To base existence on work is as stupid as to found society on economic principles. Love of the task makes work joyful, and a good economic order is a secondary result. Mechanicalness, the emanation of a warped consciousness, as well as valueless money, these have been the cause and means of action for ambitious leaders to drag our world into the depths of misery.

Out of this comes a reaction which will betray the expectations of these misguiding masters. The divine spark ever slumbers in man, and when animated by a new breath, it is irresistible.

We have attempted here to set forth some ideas on the meaning of esoterism; there are no words to make it clearer. Often, the ideas are neither explained nor even connected: accept the fact it is well that it should be so.

As for words, their meaning must sometimes be read in different ways: the language of the *medu-Neter* is not in the dictionary of mummified ideas.

The philosophers of modern times will find it difficult to agree on the sense in which words such as "intelligence," "reason," "understanding," "consciousness," and so forth, are to be taken. Their thought does not lack for power and subtlety, but they have no knowledge of genesis.

In order to expand the vocabulary, ideas must spring from consciousness. Thus it is useless to attempt to enrich our collection of meaningless words, even if the need be felt.

Our philosophers can elaborate philosophical systems and carry analysis as far as they like; yet, in order to surmount the obstacles before them, they will always be forced to resort to faith (undemonstrable affirmation), or else to negation. The latter course is the easier, and appeals to the partisans of laziness and impotence, who express it through atheism or rationally justified indifference.

All speculative philosophy is in vain; any explanation of life, of its origin and end, can never be more than the circling of a central point which is logically undefinable. Such a search is not sterile but must cease when reason acquires the certainty that this point exists. Otherwise, it will surely become a wandering in a fog of suppositions along a thousand paths leading to nowhere.

How then to express oneself clearly?

By image and by myth, as the sages of all times have done. The most subtle way of speaking the truth is to be found in the pure doctrine of the Tao; but apart from the general directives stemming from it, the *Tao Te Ching* is inaccessible even to the most erudite Chinese of our day. A symbolic (even hieroglyphic) principle guided the establishment of the Chinese ideogram, and therein may be found the esoteric expression. The latter has been lost in adopting the ideogramic convention, just as hieratic script causes its hieroglyphic origin to be forgotten in the alphabetic adaptations deriving therefrom.

Everywhere else, we find myth: Brahmanic, Judaic, Christian.

May Christians not accuse us of trying to deny the existence of a historical reality. From our point of view, myth is a reality, not a convention. It is the representation of the natural principle, which it cannot be "in truth" without resorting to the natural fact. That this principle should then assume a *synthesis form*, that is, become an incarnation, is not in the least extraordinary. The thinking of an epoch—its character—is not a fluid flung in all directions of space. It is the Idea which cannot be situated, which assumes a mental and also a bodily form when the instrument for its manifestation is given through preparation, namely, intelligence-of-the-heart and cosmic genesis. Thus the Idea springs forth in the form of ideas on all sides, simultaneously.

The end of Pharaonic Egypt is *the end of a cosmic cycle*, and not the end of a kingdom. Osiris, through Isis-Mary, engendered Horus-Christ, already announced, contained, and known in Pharaonic esoterism. The time (phase of the cosmic genesis) having arrived with the sign of Pisces the Fish, the Divine Child is born. He is born of spirit, he is born of the necessity engendered by the fall of the Word into matter. In Nature, by the rotation of the world's cycles and by means of mental knowledge, the rupture of primordial equilibrium becomes self-consciousness, the conscious at-one-ment of Being within itself. What was virtual became actual through the fulfillment of all possible aspects of the form. But Joshua-Jesus fell from heaven in the full perfection of Nature's final form,

and this is the herald of an End.

Luxor, Egypt
Christmas 1947

A note on the works of
R.A. AND ISHA SCHWALLER DE LUBICZ

After many years of studying the medieval legacy in religious, Hermetic, and esoteric fields, and their manifestation in the Gothic cathedrals, R.A. and Isha Schwaller de Lubicz experienced a recognition of that same expression in the monuments of the Pharaohs.

Their work represents the first important breakthrough in our comprehension of Egypt since Champollion deciphered the Rosetta Stone. This penetration of the monuments' symbolism and their intuitive reading of the glyphs situates Egypt, not Greece, as the cradle of our Western heritage. The de Lubiczs' work serves as a guide that will initiate the reader into the authentic tone, structure, and mentality of Egyptian wisdom.

Both R.A. and Isha Schwaller de Lubicz were masters of a broad spectrum of knowledge. Yet it is not the de Lubiczs' grasp of the many departments of knowledge alone which is masterful, but their transcendent understanding which qualifies them to question the achievements of our civilization. The work of R.A. and Isha Schwaller de Lubicz offers direction not only to the spiritual seeker, but to the scientist and the philosopher as well.

"As a contemporary renaissance man, R.A. Schwaller de Lubicz, who in his youth studied painting with Matisse, may fall into that category of genius shared by such luminaries as Rudolf Steiner and Emanuel Swedenborg. He combined the talents of social reformer, artist, scientist, visionary, and mystic to formulate ideas that were so far ahead of their time they seemed doomed, until recently, to be ignored."

EastWest

BOOKS OF RELATED INTEREST

Symbol and the Symbolic
Ancient Egypt, Science, and the Evolution of Consciousness
by R. A. Schwaller de Lubicz

The Temple of Man
by R. A. Schwaller de Lubicz

The Temples of Karnak
by R. A. Schwaller de Lubicz
Photographs by Georges and Valentine de Miré

A Study of Numbers
A Guide to the Constant Creation of the Universe
by R. A. Schwaller de Lubicz

The Egyptian Miracle
An Introduction to the Wisdom of the Temple
by R. A. Schwaller de Lubicz
Illustrated by Lucie Lamy

The Temple in Man
Sacred Architecture and the Perfect Man
by R. A. Schwaller de Lubicz
Illustrated by Lucie Lamy

Sacred Science
The King of Pharaonic Theocracy
by R. A. Schwaller de Lubicz

The Opening of the Way
A Practical Guide to the Wisdom Teachings of Ancient Egypt
by Isha Schwaller de Lubicz

Awakening Higher Consciousness
Guidance from Ancient Egypt and Sumer
by Lloyd M. Dickie and Paul R. Boudreau

The Golden Number
Pythagorean Rites and Rhythms in the Development
of Western Civilization
by Matila C. Ghyka
Introduction by Paul Valéry

Point of Origin
Gobekli Tepe and the Spiritual Matrix
for the World's Cosmologies
by Laird Scranton

The Mystery of Skara Brae
Neolithic Scotland and the Origins of Ancient Egypt
by Laird Scranton

The Cosmological Origins of Myth and Symbol
From the Dogon and Ancient Egypt
to India, Tibet, and China
by Laird Scranton

The Science of the Dogon
Decoding the African Mystery Tradition
by Laird Scranton

Sacred Symbols of the Dogon
The Key to Advanced Science in the
Ancient Egyptian Hieroglyphs
by Laird Scranton

The Sirius Mystery
New Scientific Evidence
of Alien Contact 5,000 Years Ago
by Robert Temple

Esoteric Egypt
The Sacred Science of the Land of Khem
by J. S. Gordon

Inner Traditions • Bear & Company
P.O. Box 388
Rochester, VT 05767
1-800-246-8648
www.InnerTraditions.com

Or contact your local bookseller